I Thought You Would Be Funnier

I THOUGHT YOU WOULD BE FUNNIER
Published by BOOM! Town,
an imprint of BOOM! Studios.

Copyright © 2010 Shannon Wheeler.

Office of publication: 6310 San Vicente Blvd, Ste 404, Los Angeles, CA 90048-5457.

A catalog record for this book is available from OCLC and on our website
www.boom-studios.com
on the Librarians page.

More information about and work by Shannon Wheeler can be found at his website here:
www.tmcm.com
You can contact Shannon Wheeler at: cartoons@tmcm.com
Find some of these cartoons and more at: www.act-i-vate.com

FIRST EDITION

I Thought You Would Be Funnier

SHANNON WHEELER

Introduction *by* DAN PIRARO

BOOM! Town is an imprint of BOOM! Studios

❧ INTRODUCTION ❧

FOR MY MONEY, NO GRAPHIC ART FORM SAYS MORE ABOUT HUMAN CREATIVITY THAN THE SINGLE PANEL COMIC. Though as a kid I read and enjoyed comic strips in the daily paper, as soon as I discovered magazine cartoons, I was hooked for life. How many gags have been done about psychiatrist's offices or a lone person stuck on a tiny island? How many different things can be said about someone walking a dog or a couple lying in bed? Yet these premises remain a constant source of inspiration for hundreds if not thousands of cartoons every year. I've done hundreds on these topics myself but I still regularly run across original takes that make me smile or, more painfully, that I wish I'd thought of myself. Shannon Wheeler has this gift and there are more than a few cartoons in this collection for which I will hate him for years.

Long-form comics can be just as funny or poignant, of course, as we've seen in Shannon's classic *Too Much Coffee Man* series. While making a joke in 3, 6, or 9 panels may seem the same as making one in a single panel, it is very different. In longer comics, you have time to set up a gag, build a story, say something about the characters that adds to the punch line. Even in single panel comics with regular characters, like *Family Circus*, *Dennis the Menace*, or *Marmaduke*, you are able to rely on the reader's knowledge of the characters. But in the one-off-single-glimpse-out-of-nowhere cartoon, all of that must be done in a few words and a single momentary glimpse in time. It is a unique skill and one that is particularly satisfying to the human brain. As we look at the picture and read the caption, we must perform a little mental gymnastic that tells us who these people are, what happened just before this moment, or what is about to happen after it. And we do it in a matter of a couple of seconds or less. The result is a satisfying feeling that we are in some sort of club. And that fun comes just from reading it. Writing a gag like this is exhilarating.

It is to our society's great shame that so few venues remain for this kind of humor. When I was a kid in the late 1900s, virtually every magazine was littered with single panel cartoons. In those days, a freelance gag cartoonist could make a decent living with just the sort of work that fills this book. For some inexplicable, dark and mysterious reason (I'm guessing Dick Cheney had something to do with it) only *The New Yorker* has continued this tradition. This leaves far too many talented cartoonists and far too few places to pay their creators what they are worth. People like Shannon Wheeler are paupers as a result, scribbling cartoons with fingerless gloves on found pieces of paper and shredded cardboard, sleeping on sidewalks outside the offices of the few editors who still buy single panel gags. Even though he can do something that brings joy to millions, he is shunned as an untouchable.

People who can think this way, who can sum up the human condition or comment on the ludicrous, the unjust, the absurd, the banal and ubiquitous in one surreal, inspired stroke of art and words that makes us laugh are to be cherished and revered. People like Shannon Wheeler are national treasures and no matter how much money they are making, it isn't half enough.

Okay, I added that last paragraph because I do this for a living, too.

—DAN PIRARRO
Creator of the internationally renowned
single panel gag strip *Bizarro*

Love & Relationships

"Fetch!"

"Here's one: 'an unattractive incompetent man seeks an attractive bitchy woman for a sitcom-type relationship.'"

"If you had told me you were a werewolf,
of course I would have told you I was a vampire."

"Is this the ex-girlfriend with the low self-esteem or the funny boobs?"

"Do you, SWF, take this SWM for a long-term monogamous,
mutually supportive, emotionally honest relationship?"

"It's late, we're tired, and I'm a little bit drunk.
I think it's a good time to talk about our relationship."

"I don't blame you for all our problems,
I just blame you for all our problems that remind me of my parents."

"I'm looking for that special someone to hate."

"Honestly? I prefered it when we didn't talk about the elephant."

"We're getting hyphenated."

"I can't figure you out. Your shirt says educated, but your hat says ignorant."

"It's not you, it's me."

Death & Clowns

"*It always creeps me out when you work the circus.*"

"It hurts when I laugh."

"At least we know the condom worked."

17

"Maybe you can tell me, is it spelled sithe or scythe?"

"I feel like you're not taking me seriously as a boss."

"*I thought you would be funnier.*"

"*Laughter is the best medicine, unless of course, you need your heart medicine.*"

"Does this smell funny to you?"

Kids & Life

John wore the same clothes his whole life.
He was stylish, not stylish, stylish, not stylish, stylish, not stylish,
stylish, not stylish, stylish.

"I'd be more nostalgic if I weren't so senile."

"I'm saving candy now for retirement."

"We're hoping for an overachiever."

"Are you ready for your power nap?"

"You divide the blocks and I'll draw up the papers."

"It's a _play_ date. You don't go to second base."

"*I don't know what's wrong. He's potty trained but he'll only pee on trees.*"

"Mom, Dad, please don't be mad. I want to get a tattoo removed."

"*Can I call you back?*"

Coffee & Booze

"$47.50, please."

"I want Happiness...wait, no, Ecstacy...or
maybe Peace...Serenity. I want Serenity!"

"I hate all these people."

"*Tell me again the difference between a cappuccino and a latte.*"

"You'll have to speak up. Everyone is on their cell phone."

"*I find it lowers expectations.*"

"I'm waiting for a job that covers my self-medication."

"Half-empty. Yours?"

"Writing a will is just giving up all hope of living forever."

The Last Call.

Art & Inspiration

Writing is 90% procrastination and 30% panic.

"*Why can't you be more like your fiction?*"

"*A memoir should not be about writing your autobiography.*"

"If only I'd started procrastinating last week."

"I'm writing an autobiography and he's working on the sequel."

"*Stop mocking me!*"

"We never should have encouraged him to express himself."

"It's practical, but it lacks that certain elegance."

"He's a non-graphic novelist."

"'L'esprit d'escalier!' <u>That's</u> the expression I couldn't think of."

"I can't do anything before I've had my coffee."

"*I just don't feel very omnipotent today.*"

"*Kilroy, stop looking over that fence!*"

Business & Busybodies

"*Don't be silly. You're not fired. You're un-hired.*"

Sisyphus gets a government job.

"Actually, most of us are here dropping off job applications."

"I want you to think of me not as your boss, but as someone who has absolute control of your livelihood."

"It's official. We're desperate."

"Have a seat."

"I'd go crazy, but I don't think my insurance covers it."

Enhanced job interview techniques.

"I'm still not sure how I went from self-employed to self-unemployed."

"You'll be taking Patrick's place."

"I hate materialism, but I hate not having stuff even more."

"*Would you like some pepper on your loan?*"

Law & Medicine

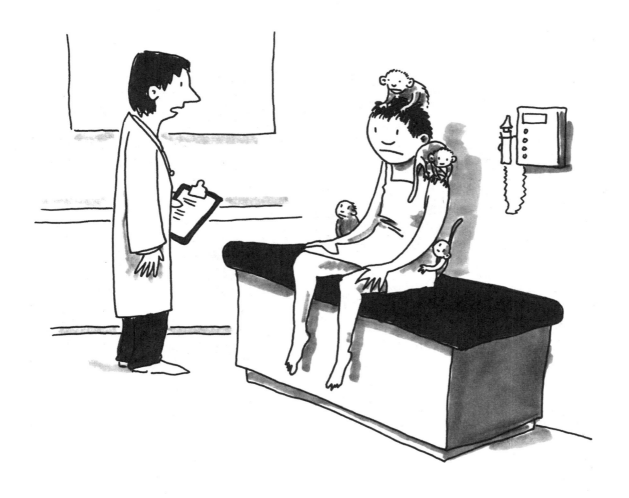

"You have monkeys."

"J'accuse!"

"So when she said 'duck' I assumed she was flirting."

"Tell me, how long have you felt like an imaginary patient?"

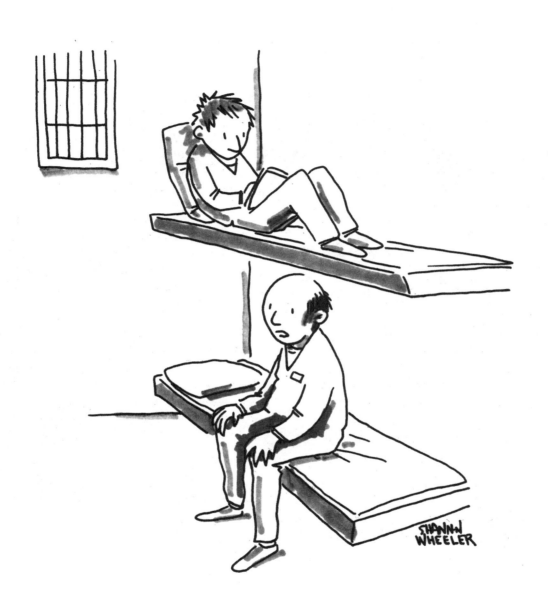

"I miss moral ambiguity."

"Honey, wake up! The lawyers are back."

"Just relax. This won't hurt a bit."

"Could someone help me?"

"Then the judge said we'd just have to agree to disagree."

78

"There's a ruling I didn't expect."

"Stop me if you've heard this one before."

The Big Picture

"Someday, none of this will be yours."

"Is there even that much of a market for large collided haldons anyway?"

"Here, let me kill our conversation by looking it up on Wikipedia."

"*I should have known it was over when she unfriended me.*"

"No Googling!"

"Look at this. I found a great little bistro on the Lower East Side."

"Imagine how much faster this would be if we had computers."

"*That beard makes you look like a terrorist.*"

"I give symbolically."

"Tell me that story where you have a job and all the bills are paid."

"I had that nightmare about chotchkies again."

"I don't care if it was on sale."

"I'm sorry to hear about your son, Mrs. Dumpty."

Cats & Dogs

"Faster. She's gaining!"

"I'm tired of chewing shoes. I'm thinking of going back to school."

"*Park!*"

"I want a job helping people... preferably something that involves sitting on laps."

"You've proven yourself the best wrangler ever and, better yet,
you can get rid of those mice you herded last week."

"*He sounds great, but you have to ask yourself, can a schnauzer really make you happy?*"

"It turns out you can buy them at the pet store."

"You don't chase me as much as you used to."

"I used to be an Egyptian God. Now I'm just a guy with a dog's head."

"My cats are more WTF than LOL."

"Go ahead, ask him anything you want about dogs."

"She misses the fish."

"I can't help it. I love to fetch."

"You know where I could buy a flying cat?"

And so the "Great Couch Treaty of 2010" was reached.

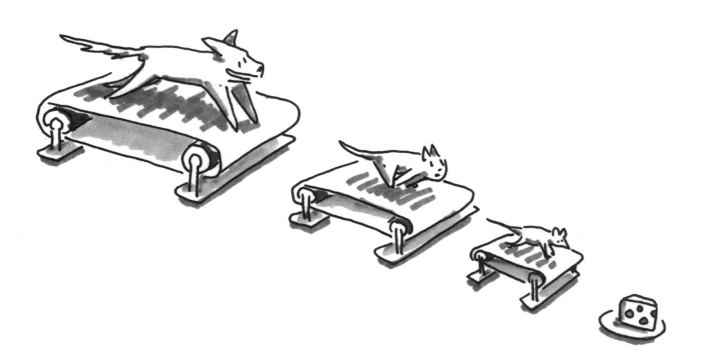

Special Thanks:

Patricia Wheeler, Richard Epstein, Austin, Berkeley, Ariel, Maria and Max.

And Matt Diffee and Bob Mankoff at The New Yorker.